Also by August Kleinzahler

HOLLYHOCKS IN THE FOG

AUGUST KLEINZAHLER

—

HOLLYHOCKS IN THE FOG

—

SELECTED SAN FRANCISCO POEMS

—

FARRAR STRAUS GIROUX / NEW YORK

Farrar, Straus and Giroux
18 West 18th Street, New York 10011

Most of the poems in this book originally appeared, some in different form, in the following publications: the *London Review of Books*, *The New Yorker*, *The Threepenny Review*, and *The Times Literary Supplement*. Several of the poems also appeared in the collections *The Hotel Oneira*, *Sleeping It Off in Rapid City*, and *Live from the Hong Kong Nile Club*.

Library of Congress Cataloging-in-Publication Data
Names: Kleinzahler, August, author.
Title: Before dawn on bluff road : selected New Jersey poems ;
    Hollyhocks in the fog : selected San Francisco poems / August Kleinzahler.
Description: First edition. | New York : Farrar, Straus and Giroux, 2017.
Identifiers: LCCN 2016041349 | ISBN 9780374282110 (hardcover) |
    ISBN 9780374715946 (e-book)
Subjects: | BISAC: POETRY / American / General.
Classification: LCC PS3561.L38285 A6 2017b | DDC 811/.54—dc23
LC record available at https://lccn.loc.gov/2016041349

Designed by Quemadura

Our books may be purchased in bulk for promotional, educational, or business use. Please contact your local bookseller or the Macmillan Corporate and Premium Sales Department at 1-800-221-7945, extension 5442, or by e-mail at MacmillanSpecialMarkets@macmillan.com.

www.fsgbooks.com
www.twitter.com/fsgbooks
www.facebook.com/fsgbooks

10 9 8 7 6 5 4 3 2 1

TO MARCY,

"YOU'RE THE BEST BREAK THIS OLD HEART EVER HAD"

—RECORDED BY ED BRUCE; U.S. BILLBOARD
HOT COUNTRY SINGLES, #1, MARCH 1982

IL EST AMER ET DOUX, PENDANT LES NUITS D'HIVER,
D'ÉCOUTER, PRÈS DU FEU QUI PALPITE ET QUI FUME,
LES SOUVENIRS LOINTAINS LENTEMENT S'ÉLEVER
AU BRUIT DES CARILLONS QUI CHANTENT DANS LA BRUME.

—CHARLES BAUDELAIRE, "LA CLOCHE FÊLÉE"

CONTENTS

HOLLYHOCKS IN THE FOG

HOLLYHOCKS IN THE FOG

Every evening smoke blows in from the sea, sea
smoke, ghost vapor
of lost frigates, sunken destroyers.
It hangs over the eucalyptus grove,
cancels the hills,
curls around garbage sacks outside the lesbian bar.

And every evening the black bus arrives,
the black *Information* bus from down the Peninsula,
unloading the workers at the foot of the block.
They wander off, this way and that, into the fog.
Young, impassive, islanded within their tunes:
Death Cab for Cutie, Arcade Fire . . .

From this distance they seem almost suspended,
extirpated, floating creatures of exile,
as they walk past the Victorian facades
and hollyhocks in their fenced-in plots,
red   purple   apricot
solitary as widows or disgraced metaphysicians.

Perhaps they're exhausted, overwhelmed by it all:
spidering the endless keywords, web pages,
appetite feeding on itself:

frantic genealogists, like swarms of killer bees.
The countless, urgent inquiries:
the poor *Cathars* and the *Siege of Carcassonne*—

what can these long-ago misfortunes tell us of ourselves, of life—
Epinephrine-induced response,
Ryne Duren + wild pitches + 1958 . . .
Knowledge a trembling Himalayas of rubble:
Huitzilopochtli, Chubby Checker . . .
But for now they are done, till the bus comes again tomorrow.

There is nothing further to be known.
The fog, like that animate *nothingness*
of Lao-tzu's sacred Tao,
has taken over the world, and, with night settling in,
all that had been, has ever been, is gone,
gone but for the sound of the wind.

BAY LULLABY

Tuesdays are bad for sausage and flowers,
rain
sweeping in off the sea, foghorns
lowing like outsize beasts
shackled to cliffs at the mouth of the Bay.

You hear them from under the movie marquee
before going in to dry
off in plush, alone
behind two old ladies, that song of a wanton from long ago,
"Temptation," filling the empty room.

Across the city's northwest quadrant,
two, maybe three miles in,
drifting through holes in the traffic and rain,
you hear them warning ships off the rocks,
moaning like fettered gods.

Lilies begun to curl
and meat gone sad at the delicatessen,
trays of *wurst*,
fat seeping into the skins
before Thursday delivery and the big weekend.

As morning's first trolley clears the track,
the cat's petite snores,
my love's upper lip beaded with sweat,
you can still hear them,
out there in the dark,
mingling their calls in the rain.

LAND'S END

This air,
you say, *feels as if it hasn't touched land*
for a thousand miles,

as surf sound washes through scrub
and eucalyptus,
whether ocean or wind in the trees

or both: the park's big windmill
turning overhead
while joggers circle the ball field

only a few yards off
this path secreted in growth and mist,
the feel of a long narrow theater set

about it here on the park's western edge
just in from the highway
then the moody swells of the Pacific.

The way the chill goes out of us
and the sweat comes up
as we drive back into the heat

and how I need to take you
to all the special places, or show
you where the fog rolls down

and breaks apart in these hills or where
that gorgeous little piano bridge
comes halfway through the song,

because when what has become dormant,
meager, or hardened
passes through the electric

of you, the fugitive scattered pieces
are called back to their nature—
light pouring through muslin

in a strange, bare room.

SUMMER JOURNAL

[3 p.m.]

Loss leaders in shop windows,
fog spilling down the slopes
of Corona Heights, Twin Peaks, Tank Hill—

my name on everyone's lips:

—*August*, they say,
with resignation and dismay,
pulling up their collars against the wind.

[Blue]

The student doctors in blue scrubs,
passing up and down Parnassus to the hospital,
now invisible, on top of the hill,

past the bougainvilleas and kebab shop:

eighteen-, thirty-hour shifts, back and forth,
out on their feet, ghostly in the fog.

"Coming Up the Hudson,"
the altered title of an old Monk tune—

why, when the interns and residents drift by,
must it be these particular words that assemble in my mind?

[*L'Art poétique*]

—*Just let it sit there for a while cooking in its own juices,*

my father used to say
of a dish newly taken hot from the oven.

[*Garden Out Back Window*]

White, the jasmine and magnolia,
set off by the dark green shellac of its leaves;
red, the trumpet vine winding up the palm,
fuchsia and tequila sage;
the orange nasturtium flower, marmalade bush
in flame;
and Hooker's evening primrose:

the sphinx moth at dusk, the hummingbirds
dipping into its nectar wells,

the goldfinch visiting for its black seeds;
bright yellow,
the color heightened in gray light—

neon along the fogbound Ginza.

[Map]

On the wall of the darkened hallway,
not long before dawn,
horns baying out by the rocks
muffled by fog—
"All Blues" played through a Harmon mute . . .

Europa, the wild dog,
her snout in the Pyrenees, licks clean
the Gouffre de la Pierre-Saint-Martin
below the Pic d'Arles,

knocking sideways the steeples
of Zaragoza,

then slobbering into the Río Jalón.

[Golden Gate]

Two turkey vultures, wings unfurled like spinnakers,
dry and groom themselves,
late morning atop Yellow Bluff.

The decks of the bridge vibrate:
El Caminos, Acuras, Cabriolets—

within their plastic and metal housings,
sentient beings,

in whose own housings, brainpans, and soft tissue,
imaginings, dreams, the phantom conversations
are played and replayed.

Diadems, crab mites, worm larvae in the Bay below . . .

—Subhuti, are there many particles of dust
in the three thousand chiliocosms?

Very many, World-Honored One.

[Tuesday]

The same, and the same again . . .

The oboist upstairs—
why does he insist on practicing during my afternoon nap?

Why does it always have to be Ravel?

[Snowy Plover]

Snowy plovers
hopping this way and that in the wet sand,

skirmishing, posturing, poking around for bugs.

The vast, bruise-colored fogbank
sitting out there,
spread across the horizon like some dreadful prophecy
waiting to blow in.

New York, London—
a great busyness and agitation in the streets,
offices, gathering places

among those who truly matter,
assembling that day's world, disassembling it,
commenting at length on same.

[Cloud Forest]

I took him up to the Cloud Forest,
just behind the Medical Center.
Snails crunched in the soft duff underfoot.
This upset him.
Water dripping from the eucalyptus;
The sharp tap-tap of a downy woodpecker,
its sound reverberating among the treetops.

—Ischi, Issa, Issa, Ischi.

Try saying that ten times fast as you can.
The haiku master in his quilted priest robes,
the "last wild Indian" in his bark knickers.
They took a good long look at each other.
Actually, they could well have passed for brothers,
the heathen fitter and darker
by several shades. Gentle sorts, the two of them,
and taciturn as can be. No harm there;
not like an Algonquin Round Table was on tap.

Can't really say what I reckoned was on tap.
Ischi, since they first smoked him out,
behind the slaughterhouse over in Oroville,
this is now his place, his home.
Every so often they come up the hill and fetch him:
some big-shot out-of-town phrenologist
wanting to whip out the calipers, poke him, make him say *ahhh*.
Otherwise, they leave him be,
happy as Larry with his grubs and chipmunks and handicrafts.

Issa much taken with the yellow banana slugs:
Readers will well know how he feels about gastropods,
fifty-four haiku devoted to the snail alone.

The two of them seem to be hitting it off,
in their quiet way, just sitting there on a log,
the one whittling away, the other staring at the ground.
Don't even seem aware that I'm around.

[Dead Zone]

The *dead zone*—

headlights catch the fog pooling round the tires
of oncoming traffic.

All-Star break, midsummer,
football still eight weeks away:
you hear it in the voice of the radio sports-talk host,

the pitch half an octave higher,
the rush of words, the combativeness,
no one calling in but the hard cases,

the same sad, old bachelors,
chewing the cud, chewing the cud, chewing . . .

[Wind / Work]

The sound of the wind awakens me,
I cannot say what time,
but in the depths of night.
I can tell by the absence of street noise.

The gusts seem to arrive in sequences of three,
two short, one long—
violent anapests, the last the most protracted
and fierce,
gaining in force over its duration,
tossing the big palm's crown of fronds
until they crackle,
bending back the top of its trunk.
The building itself trembles.

Then a few minutes of calm until the next rush
of wind, each sequence more intense
than the last until it finally blows itself out.

I lie there struggling to remember a word.
It takes a while,
but it's not far. As I begin to doze off
it comes to me,
as so many things do in this condition of mind.

Zamboni

Just the word,
not the ice-restoring machine of hockey arenas,
or Mr. Zamboni of Paramount, California,
and his ungainly, lucrative invention.

It was necessary that I find the word.
Whatever else happens in the course of the day,
the important work has been done.

[Cabinet of Timbres]

From my Cabinet of Timbres
I remove two viols, one treble, one bass, a theorbo,
chitarrone, violin, and, bless her,
here comes Ludmilla from the front room
wheeling the chamber organ down the hall.

I draw my bath,
as I do every morning this time of year
with the world outside having disappeared
but for the greenery out back, foregrounded,
bobbing and trembling in the stiff sea wind.

I shall have my chord,
even if I have to sit here soaking in this dark room
the entire morning.
                    Schmelzer, Biber, Kapsberger—
it's in there somewhere

among the toccatas, sonatas, chaconnes.
I know because I have heard it there before.

A HISTORY OF WESTERN MUSIC: CHAPTER 29

IN MEMORIAM THOM GUNN
(AFTER JOHNNY MERCER)

I took a trip on a plane
And I thought about you
I lunched alone in the rain
And I thought about you

One streetcar, then two, disappearing from view
A tortured dream
The fog blowing in, canceling all that had been
Going street by street
Like a cop on his beat

Over the Great Salt Lake
Yeah, I thought about you
But when I pulled down the shade
Man, I really got blue

I snuck a peak at the clouds
Muttered something aloud
Something I once said to you

We do as we have to
I thought about you

THE SINGLE GENTLEMAN'S
CHOW MEIN

The ants are very bad tonight
and the poison is old.
It's the rains that bring them out,
you know. The first big storm
and there they are,
all over the counter and with their scouts
in advance, under the sink mat
and mason jars, probing
the way they do.

They have a smell, of that I'm certain,
a formic aroma,
that gathers around them in the heat
of their frenzy; I don't know
but that they take it on outside
and bring it in along with them
on their journeys through these walls.

But they do enjoy it, the bait.
It must still have some strength.
See how they cluster.
You need only stir the paste
with the end of a match

and the arsenic's perfume blooms again.
They really do love it.
Watch how they feed.
Soon they will take the poison back
from where they have come,
back to their nest,
and destroy their queen.

I only ordered half a pound this time.
Most evenings—yes, most—
I would probably get a whole and leave some
for lunch next day,
perhaps a casserole.
But just tonight it was looking,
well, a trifle sad,
sitting up there in its steam tray
for half an eternity.

You know how it tends to get slow
after the lunch trade.
The one batch sits in its grease for hours,
taking on that viscous, cloudy look,
almost jaundiced under the fluorescent lights.
From time to time the homeless wander in
and bargain for some rice,
perhaps a spear of wilted broccoli.
And if it's quiet, the Lotus will oblige.

But I do like it.
I add things on, you see:
vegetables, all manner of condiments
and treats, a shrimp
or scallop, or two, or three.
It's very nice the way I do it,
and never the same way twice.

They know me down there,
at the Lotus, I mean,
and have done for years.
The girls behind the counter change.
—*Ah, ha, chow mein,*
they say, smiling when they remember me.
It's quite nice, really.
One of them, oh, three years back
was a stunner, terribly pretty;
taking a night course, as I recall.
—*You look like professor, no?*
she said to me one day, a trifle severe
in delivery but very sweet.
I've never been with a Chinese.

NOIR

The light emission diodes stare,
incandescent crab eyes.
Foghorns trade calls in the night
as if lost, seeking one another out,
sometimes in the key of A,
sounding out there by the cliffs,
sometimes in G or C,
depending on how the fog is blowing,
but always at their loudest right before dawn.

A fine rain falls.
The actors scuttle back to their trailers
after the hours of hitting their spots,
muffed scenes, take after take,
shivering out there under the helium lamps.
Another crap, over-budget homage
to Hammett and John Alton,
Magyar master of the shadow game:
fog, steam, and smoke,
bad news behind the slatted blinds,
the half-illumined face
and pistol's report.

Exhausted, feeling a little debauched
after too much weasel, cop and tough, good-time Mabel,
down on her luck,
the canny Chinaman named Wu,
three of them play cards,
the other two, after a few lines of blow, screw.

The front is blowing in from the south.
You can taste it in the air,
smell it.
The flags on the downtown buildings begin to snap.
It starts out there on the Pacific,
a thousand miles off the China coast,
and comes across on the westerlies.
That's what it does this time of year.
I've been out here a long time.
Every year.
You can set your clock by it.

SUNSET IN CHINATOWN

The massive cable turns on its spool, pulling
carloads of tourists to the city's crest

             as the sun sits low
in the hills above Chinatown, exploding

suddenly in the window of Woey Loy Meats, high
along the top of the glass,

showering light over barbecued ducks—

a somehow elegiac splash
this evening, the last week before Labor Day

as if summer, in tandem with the sun,
were being pulled down

and away from us by the great spool's turning.

Thus, the sullen old man in his Mao cap
plucks the zither for change

on a crate outside the gewgaw shop:

first, the ancient "Song of Cascading Water,"
followed by the plaintive
                    "Lament of the Empress Ch'ou"

and even the bad little boy from Wichita Falls
trailing behind his parents in a sulk

registers that twinge

birds in the sky, insects and beasts no less
than the immortals

feel

when the plangent notes take shape in the air,
aligning their souls with Heaven and Earth.

SEPTEMBER

The long-beleaguered home team,
black hats and orange piping,
is eliminated on a cool night,
the very end of September,
with the *phlox* zerspalten *by rain*,
as Benn wrote,
and *giving forth a strange animal smell*,
seltsamen Wildgeruchs.

While the neighboring team
from across the Bay,
the ones with green leggings,
younger and more brazen,
were finished earlier still, after the clamor
attending their midsummer surge.

Frucht und Fieberschwellungen
abfallend . . .
                    Even the strongest
of young arms
tires over a long season.
Tumescences of fruit and fever . . .
Knees give out, just as the parapets
of Troy rear into sight.

What do the sky and gardens know
of such disappointments?
Of the quiet on the street,
life ebbing from barrooms like a yeasty tide?
Go home, everyone, go home.
The cupped flame,
the extended sigh of smoke in the shadows
of a hundred doorways.
Go home to your wives, go home.

Why must it always end this way,
every year the same?
It is only we who change, Time
eroding our powers—
des Sommers Narr, Nachplapperer,
summer's fool, night jabberer—
putting to rout our boyish hopes.

And even with the air so sharp
once night has settled in—
vor dir der Schnee, Hochschweigen—
when the season's first hearth fires
mingle their exhalations
with night-blooming vegetation,
snow and silence ahead of you,

the sun next day pours down
with such intent as if it could surpass
what only it might emulate,
its counterfeit betrayed
by the very merest wash of bronze

enveloping the Chinese lantern,
jasmine, and flowering lavender
in a memorial glow
while, still, they bloom, thrive, reach
up, upward, toward the light
and out from amid the withered stalks and ruin
of what summer has left behind.

INDIAN SUMMER NIGHT:
THE HAIGHT

The 43 bus at Carl & Cole
steps on the comic's line
but applause and laughter
waft up the lane.
A *ranger* on the grass
bestirs himself,
spooked

then barks back a laugh of his own,
an unwholesome laugh,
stiffening the neighbor cats.

The summer my sister worked at Palisades Park
I'd stay awake till midnight
listening.
When the breeze in the maple was right
you could hear her,

my sister,
over the loudspeakers a quarter mile away
telling the barkers, patrons, and freaks,

everybody,
the last voice before the lights went out,

—*Thank you. Good night.*

PEACHES IN NOVEMBER

Peaches redden,
and at day's end glow as if from within
the way bronze does,

before thudding down.
Mourning doves scatter at the sound,
shooting away in low trajectories,

and the mind starts,
in spite of itself, even after weeks
of hearing them drop through the night

and all day long:
the intervals so far off any possible grid
of anticipation, and the impact

each time they hit
ground amid a racket of leaves
just different enough

from the time before,
and the time before that, you are tricked
out of thought, awake

to the sound
as the last of them come down
and the boughs slowly raise themselves up.

LATE INDIAN SUMMER

The rains hold off another week,
and the midday heat,
long after the wine grapes are in, has the cat
sprawled flat under the jade plant.

Nights already belong to winter.
You know by that tuning fork in its jacket
of bone
broadcasting to the body's far ports.

Days like this so late in the year
inflame desire, perturb
the ground of dreams, and roust us from sleep,
exhausted and stunned.

THE SWIMMER

The japonica and laurels tremble
as the wind picks up
out the west-facing wall of the old natatorium,
made wholly of glass.
The swimmer takes her laps,
steady but sure through a blur of turquoise
and importunings of chlorine.
The large room itself now darkens,
lit as it is by natural light,
as the storm clouds press closer toward land.

Back and forth, the solitary swimmer,
now on her second mile,
is caught up, held almost,
in that one element she finds her ease;
and in moving through it
the very edges of her strength are engaged,
until, on a turn, her breathing stretched,
health pours into her.

The great glass wall, first pilloried by drops,
their dull, pellet-like clack,
is now streaming with rain:
and from this hill

where, half-hidden, the old rec center sits,
across the sixty rolling blocks to the sea,
all that is material and solid,
the houses, the cars, the trees,
diminish into shadow
and continue to recede till there is nothing,
nothing at all in the world,
but water.

SUNDAY IN NOVEMBER

And who were they all in your sleep last night
    chattering so
you'd think that when you woke
the living room would be full of friends and ghosts?

But you see, nobody's here, no one but you
    and the room's nearly bare
except for Paddy's play-string all covered in dust
and a bottle of tinted air.

Pop and Lola, the sullen little clerk from the store,
    and eight or ten more. Now
which were the dreams ones and who did you meet that was real?
You were, for the most part, you.

Such a big room: how nice to be alone in it
    with the one lit bulb and dying plant,
the day so large and gray outside,
dogs running through it in circles, buses, shouts.

And later on, where will you take her?
    Up to the rock. And what will you see there?
    Roofs and the Bay. Have you a song to sing her?
    The wind will do and she'll think it's me.

But who were they all in your sleep last night
    first one then the next
with their menace, wild semaphore, and lusts?
I hardly know where you find the strength

come morning.

FLYNN'S END

Flynn fell off the cable car
and landed on his head.
                              Poor Flynn,
hardly Flynn anymore,
in a dinghy listing to starboard.

Flynn on his stool,
holding court down the block
at The Magic Flute,
his hound at his feet while the old LPs
hissed and popped through the weekend:

Boccherini and Mississippi Fred,
the plucky chanteuse and gag tunes.

Flynn, with his mug of rum
and that faraway gaze—
a wryness at the eyes and mouth
frozen into a carapace
over some enormous hurt.

You see it in the look of old beatniks,
at their rituals
in the café and bar windows of North Beach,

solemnly playing cards at noon,
afflicted with some private wisdom
denied parturition.

Flynn, drunk and alone
in his shop weekday afternoons
with his binfuls of concerti
and wailing brass.
                    Alone with his dog
and his rum and the fog
coming in and too stiff
to get up and change the record.

And Flynn, with his secret poems
in a fancy red box,
thwarted and feverish and illustrated
by a suburban Beardsley,

whatever ache or shame
prettified, made diffuse, and tied
with a rhyme
like a ribbon around a present.

The ghost of him presiding
over those last lost afternoons
weeks after the earthquake,

laths and studs showing through
the walls, and plaster
sprinkling the ancient Vocalions.

Now a consortium's gone and bought the block
and the old place has a brand-new front
with black glass,
very minimal, very flash,
and sells computer software.

And Flynn drifts further and further to sea
in a bed for old strays at Laguna Honda.

SAN FRANCISCO / NEW YORK

A red band of light stretches across the west,
low over the sea, as we say goodbye to our friend,
Saturday night, in the room he always keeps unlit
and head off to take in the avenues,
actually take them in, letting the gables,

bay windows, and facades impress themselves,
the clay of our brows accepting the forms.
Darkness falls over the district's slow life,
miles of pastel stucco canceled,
with its small, arched doorways, second-floor businesses:

herbalists and accountants, jars
of depilatories. Such a strange calm, the days
already lengthening and asparagus
under two dollars a pound.
                                        Is New York fierce?

The wind, I mean. I dream of you in the shadows,
hurt, whimpering. But it's not like that, really,
is it? Lots of taxis and brittle fun.
We pass the shop of secondhand mystery novels.
with its ferrety customers and proprietress

behind her desk, a swollen arachnid
surrounded by murder and the dried-out glue
of old paperback bindings.

                           What is more touching
than a used bookstore on Saturday night,

dowdy clientele haunting the aisles:
the girl with bad skin, the man with a tic,
the chronic ass at the counter giving his art speech?
How utterly provincial and doomed we feel
tonight with the streetcar appearing over the rise

and at our backs the moon full in the east,
lighting the slopes of Mount Diablo
and the charred eucalyptus in the Oakland hills.
Did you see it in the East 60s
or bother to look up for it downtown?

And where would you have found it,
shimmering over Bensonhurst, over Jackson Heights?
It fairly booms down on us tonight
with the sky so clear,

                    and through us

as if these were ruins, as if we were ghosts.

DISAPPOINTMENT

A faint smell of urine
embroidering that bouquet of mold the big cushions
give off days the fog won't lift,

and a shelf of bone
growing out over the eyelids like evening's shadow
across a field of corn . . .

The whole parade
leaking out from your shoulders, bequeathing
to the groin a pang of distance;

then that metallic taste in the mouth
and a voice you had let yourself believe
was dead

close now by your ear, intimate and sweet:

   Well, well, well,
look what we have here.

AFTER LADY MURAKAMI

These sleeping used-car dealerships
and blowing wrappers

how many lost evenings
the meagerness, the waste

when suddenly the squeals
of a transvestite

about to gobble her cell phone

—

Just as I found myself
in the dentist chair

only yesterday
hands clutched against my thighs

so I find myself here
in this seat
heart in my throat

as you walk into the room

—

The cherry blossoms are late
this year

I had nearly forgotten about them

the pleasure they bring
always fresh, a delicacy to it

because the poets say so

or just because

—

I had on my favorite kimono
not the most precious

but the one that calls attention
to my eyes

yet when you turned
it was as if a thought, like a tick

had started to bite
and then changed its mind

—

Do they know who I am
these gibbering little foreigners

coarse, frenzied
like perfumed monkeys

her servant's averted eyes
dew on her sleeve and all the rest

none of it, never even heard
of Lady Murakami

as they crowd me aside
at the sale bin

EBENEEZER CALIFORNICUS

Don't make me go out eat goose
be nice get a headache
all right?
because the sun's so strong
so warm delish the back of my neck
making mutinous the wee city-states
that dot it—
goose bumps of intrigue, of the possible

Terrible people
up & down the street terrible people
smiling
    the smiles of greed
    the mooncalf's grin
    the Bob Hope Holiday Leer of Delight
the smile of the broken
hurt
    pullulating:
    not six weeks out of the can
    like drunk at 8 a.m.

    that smile

—Maddy crifmuss, brudder
Stare shhange?

             O Christ

O

    Merry WhackWhack, Mrs. QuackQuack

      Write soon

       Love

         Baby Teapot

CHRISTMAS IN CHINATOWN

They're off doing what they do
and it is pleasant to be here without them
taking up so much room.
They are safely among their own,
in front of their piles of meat, arguing
about cars and their generals,
and, of course, with the TV going all the while.

One reads that the digestive wind passed by cattle
is many times more destructive to the atmosphere
than all of the aerosol cans combined.
How does one measure such a thing?
The world has been coming to an end
for five thousand years. If not tomorrow,
surely, one day very soon.

FRIENDS THROUGH AT NEW YEAR'S: 1987

The old year's calendars flutter down
in the mist,

                    a custom here,
the countless sheets of dated memoranda
tossed from bank tower roofs

                    escorting them like pilot fish
to the street below

as friends pass through town,
the clan from Vancouver, two little girls
in tow.

                    We all watch cartoons together
in the front room as storms, one on the heels of the next,
push in from the west, rain
lashing the windows, runneling across the panes.

                    —This is worse than Vancouver,
Mom says,
but they all go to the carousel in the park anyhow
and catch cold
because the big one remembers from last time.

Another friend down from Juneau,
on his way south to Belize for the diving,
stares out the window for hours on end, drinking,

disinclined, as always, to say much,
every so often mentioning the woman back up in Sitka,
how the last letter was "odd,"
                    and her younger boy, Tom,
the way the two of them got on.

When old friends speak of the past,
the shorthand and measured silences strangely intact,
even after the years . . .

                    How well they seem to know you,
or what they remember of you,
better than family, than the dearest, most enduring of lovers,
it seems hardly possible,
so much that you yourself had forgotten,
alive in them still,

                    whose children fall asleep in your arms.

WINTER BALL

The squat man under the hoop
throws in short hooks, left-handed, right
in the dwindling sunlight as six lesbians
clown and shoot at the other end,
through a very loose game of three on three.

How pleased to be among themselves,
warm New Year's Day afternoon, neither young
nor graceful nor really good shots
but happy for the moment while a mutt
belonging to one of them runs

nearly out of its skin, so glad to be
near the action and smells, vigorous and dumb
but keeping his orbits well clear of the man
who would be a machine now if he could,
angling them in off both sides of the backboard.

You can tell this is a thing he's often done before,
the boy who'd shoot till dusk
when starlings exploded, filthy birds,
from roost to roost, gathering only to fly off
at the first sharp sound, hundreds as one.

He'd wonder where they went at night
as he played his solitary game of Round the World,
sinking shots from along the perimeter,
then the layup, then the foul.
                              So intent at it
and grave it almost seemed like more than a game
with dark coming on and the cold.

VISITS

You were speaking of your brother that night,
outside on the landing, the two of us
sharing one last smoke.
                                    I was headed east
for February and you were hoping to finish your work
and make it back to Recife in time for Carnival.

It was very late. The street was quiet and dark.
You spoke again about your brother,
always driving home from town drunk
the fifty or so kilometers along country roads,
back to the sugarcane farm.
                                          What a wonderful driver
he was, sure and alert, even when drinking,
and how well he knew those roads, but still, still,
one night . . .

            You were beautiful just then,
your face naked, luminous with feeling
for him and the sorrow you sensed in his life,
an adoring trance—
                                    when for no reason I looked up,
and right on top of us the radio tower,
soaring a thousand feet, its red beacon
pulsing across the sky.

Dizzy already from all the wine and smoke and feijoada,
you and Louisa vamping all night to the Cardoso records,
and then, my head thrown back,

                              taking in the monstrous surprise of it,
suddenly looming there above us.
I didn't know this neighborhood at night,
or had never bothered to look up.

But that's really it, after all:
like Monsieur Krivine from Lyon, the symphony conductor,
when we walked across town years ago
and admired the skyline from Russian Hill.

                              —*Magnificent*,
he gasped.
—*You enjoy tall buildings, do you?* I asked.

                              —*No, no*, he said,
the shapes they make of the sky.

WARM NIGHT IN FEBRUARY

It smells of summer out,
she said
        in Safeway's parking lot,
tilting her head up
to reach more air.

There is a kind of wave
that falls upon us
unawares.
        I cannot tell you
how it comes or when
but we are left there broken,
our voices everywhere scattered.

THE WIND IN MARCH

Tower of Texas is spurned for Defense:
a drunkard and womanizer they say of him,
a mean little man.

And a wild March wind cuts a trough
through the grass, scattering
papers, making the old palmetto weave as tourists,

shoppers, and the homeless pull up their collars,
bending into the wind, pausing an instant
as if to take measure of their gravity before going on.

One after another the headline stories are played out for us,
character and event receding
into a gray, ghostly midden dreams bubble up from

years later, dreams
from which we're awakened by the wind
spraying rain against glass, rattling

the windows in their frames. —March,
you think to yourself, trying
to remember the oddly formal little man with a drink

staring at your old girlfriend Lu
with a terrifically stagy, silent-movie sort of leer.
You were about to speak up
when the shudder and knock of wood and glass
brought you awake;
and you lie there for what seems a long time

listening to the wind, forgetting
for a minute who it is with her back pressed
against the length of you,

breathing softly.

WATCHING YOUNG COUPLES WITH AN
OLD GIRLFRIEND ON SUNDAY MORNING

How mild these young men seem to me now
with their baggy shorts and clouds of musk,
as if younger brothers of the women they escort
in tight black leather, bangs, and tattoos,
cute little toughies, so Louise Brooks annealed

in MTV, headed off for huevos rancheros
and the Sunday *Times* at some chic, crowded dive.
I don't recall it at all this way, do you?
How sweetly complected and confident they look,
their faces unclouded by the rages

and abandoned, tearful couplings of the night before,
the drunkenness, beast savor, and remorse.
Or do I recoil from their youthfulness and health?
Oh, not recoil, just fail to see ourselves.
And yet, this tenderness between us that remains

was mortared first with a darkness that got loose, a frenzy,
we still, we still refuse to name.

THE LUNATIC OF LINDLEY MEADOW

At nightfall, when the inquisitive elves in elf-pants
wander over the ridge with chummy screed,
the snaps of the beak your hand becomes cease,

and evening's last fungo dwindles
high over the spruce, for an instant getting lost
in one band of sky turning dark under another,

falling back into view, falling
out of the sky, *pop*, a dead wren in his mitt. *Let's
get home*, the big boy says, *Mom'll holler.*

The car horns along Fulton subside with the dark,
the big felt-lined dark: bright little logos and cars
set in black felt while still pulsing light,

a lid on top. And see, here he comes now,
Conga Lad, pleasing the elves, who come close but not too,
making the birds go 'way. Time to start home,

so clean it up nice and blow germs off your pouch—
the nice warm room, the smell in the wool.

ROOMS

In the sleep that finally gives rest
I take the stairs slowly
out past the azalea dell and bison paddock,

and down through these rooms once more,
this endless house
under the lawns still wet from mist,
the root systems and mulch,
only to find you at a sales counter
arguing with a Russian woman.
Her English is rough but adequate,
your argument well-reasoned, controlled.

You will in the end prevail.
The salesclerk is charmed by the snatches of Russian
you mix into the conversation,
the garment exchanged for credit.

I seldom find you in these rooms anymore,
certainly not for months.
So when our eyes meet
you look momentarily bemused,
the shiver of surprise softening to pleasure.

You are lovely,
somewhat older than I remember,
businesslike in a tailored suit.

Our conversation is courtly,
flirtatious in what we imagine an Old World way.
How strange to encounter you here
in the harsh light, the tableau
of a downtown department store with its cases
of perfumes, gels, and leather goods.
And how inexplicably refreshed I feel afterward
lying here alone,

awakened precisely as our commerce ended
by the shouts of children going to school.

THE PARK

Jimmy the Lush,
looking rough in the shadows and dapple
of light, stares down at the ground
as his dogs take command

of the boundaries,
nuzzling turds and the air around,
snouts jerking like marionettes.
He starts off slow,

nursing a Pepsi, and keeps to his post
through the morning.
He looks almost natty, frayed Ivy League,
compared with the guys

on the corner, wasted already and screaming
about which one goes
to the Arab's next to buy more beer
and some smokes.

Then comes The Talker,
muttering softly, who finds his spot
under the loquat
and fretfully grooms in the shade.

His hat could be a military beret,
but it's far too big
and he wears it wrong, puffed
high on his head like a derby

collapsed at the edges.
They usually detonate round about two,
Jimmy first, somehow
being the senior. A pint's in him now,

high-test, and he's sore
as the dickens about something.
Once it was the mayor, once the Jews,
now it's the whole stinking planet.

The sun posts west
of the radio tower and The Talker's off
on his *possessed by space-villain X* routine,
flogging his rotors, up on his feet,

while Jimmy rails on about the ozone,
the redwoods—those *bastards* . . .
He spits out the *ba* sound in *bastards*,
his voice growing louder

as his breaths get short
till there's one final shriek

and then nothing.

BACK

How familiar it all slowly becomes:
a photograph
still murky in its chemical bath;
a tune or aroma
not quite placed but close in the mind,
and then, *yes, ah, that, my my* . . .

The pastels and hills, the addled geometry—
desolation
perched on the gut like a seagull on a piling.
An outpost, by the sea,
so very far from anything and its back turned.
In defiance? Hardly.
Nothing so emphatic in this cool, silvered air.
Bewilderment, perhaps.
A studied casualness. Yes. That.

And if a woman,
beautiful, surely, at the very least,
distant, vain. But foolishly so,
endearingly.
Spaghetti straps, spike heels, and the rest.
And vague.
Ceremonially so. Stupid, maybe.
Blinkered, of course.

But handsomely turned out and well-practiced
in so very many of the comforts
that slipping away from her atmosphere
involves real pain.

One finds one's way,
slowly;
as there is no place to really hurry, is there?
Always in the small things:
a box of staples in the sideboard's drawer,
or the garlic press,
found at last behind the vinegars and pastes.
Who would have left it there?
So many people have passed through in my absence.

I have been away a long time,
Forgotten just how quiet it can seem.
No Penelope, no good blind Argos chivied by fleas.
No suitors to slay.
How terribly long it takes:
the books and closets and outside plants
finding their way back into one's head,
where and in what order.
Away for so long I'm other than I was,
having again to learn simply how to be here,
as if having another go at the piano
after how many years.

LOCK SHOP

Frank punched steel stamps into key bows
then duped them on the grinder
for thirty-odd years,
just to keep off from dead-bolt or cylinder work.
He never did learn how to locksmith—

thirty-odd years and the old nail pounder
still couldn't figure it out:
just the hammer, drill, and a big smile
for whatever lady it was up front.
Besides, he liked how hard metal bit into soft.

The last day Frank wore powder-blue Dacron slacks
And a necktie with little birds knit in.
He had coffee like always with the machinists at break,
kissed both secretaries, kissed DeLois
    at the Trouble Desk,
and left.

Now John says he's had it;
took a job in the desert down around Blythe:
a new correction facility
not a hundred miles from that land he bought
right along the Colorado.
He'll still be State so won't hurt on his pension.

John used to locksmith over at Vacaville,
"the biggest prison on earth."
Told me how the one time there he ran into Charlie Manson.
—*Was he crazy?* I asked.

—*Crazy?* John says and gives me this look.

   Crazy?

Hell yes, he was crazy.

SPRING TRANCES

Two snails have found the inside of a Granny Goose
Hawaiian-style potato chips,
the clipper ship on its wrapper
headed out from the islands

on a windswept main.
The last storms passed now, turning
to snow in the High Sierra:
they baste in their ointments deep in the tall grass,

cool among shadows and cellophane.
The sparrow and linnets have gone mad at dawn,
trilling and swooping in the branches
and ditchweed, flashing a plume

then diving; a racket
we've woken to for weeks, far too long,
before the sun turns Scotch broom and the poppies to flame.
We drift through these days

half in trance from fatigue.
At evening, as the streaks of light dissolve,
we watch the boy walk home,
hatband and uniform wet from the game.

The smell of dust and sweat and the oil in his mitt
burns deep into the tissue of him.
Buffeted, drunk, wounded—
his pretty nerves bloom,

a school of minnows just under the skin.
The wind carries music up from the street,
a skewer running through him
that he slowly turns on in the scented dark.

RAIN

(I)

The room darkens,
then darkens further with the approach
of yet another storm cell from the west
with its columns and plaits,
the tall, ghostly chambers of space between—
une fraction intense de météore pur . . .—
willow, sage, Sung green, a hint, perhaps, of Veronese;
now darkening further still
until sufficiently dark, as if at the beginning of a show,
and with the sound of it the only sound.
At which point, and not before,
might one begin to detect his outline in the rain,
like an image hidden in a picture puzzle,
slipping about, darting like a pike,
over the hoods and under the chassis of parked cars,
making an appearance in the branches
of this tree or that: immaterial, flowing, wraith-like.
His fur now grisaille, now Old Holland, then mouse,
altering in hue, just as the rain itself amidst its own shadows,
finally becoming one with the rain, and vanishing.

(II)

M. Francis Ponge, exemplar of phenomenology
and the breathing of *things*,
is sitting in the unlit front room, drapes pulled,
solemnly rapt, in the manner of a fascinated child
at home from school with the grippe.
In the distant background Señor Mompou is working through
a few sonorities—
La sonnerie au sols des filets verticaux . . .
M. Ponge is watching the entirety of Warner Bros.' *Looney Tunes,*
Vols. I and *II*, over and over, for hours on end,
while outside the rain continues to pour down.
The splashes of green, red, and yellow
jump from the screen into the darkness of the room,
attended by a battery of sound effects
mixed in with splattered chestnuts from the Romantic age.
His English is very good, impeccable, really,
but these bursts of imprecation, muttered asides,
the minatory soliloquies; these somehow defeat him utterly.

Still, his absorption is not unlike that of a scientist
examining cells which behave oddly under the microscope,
and likewise mirthless, amid an assault of mirth.

Daffy, Tweety Bird, Yosemite Sam—
each of them intriguing, but Bugs, Bugs Bunny,
having quite a time of it out there on the other side of the curtain,
is who most commands the attention of M. Ponge,
lapsed surrealist, champion of the apple
in all its apple-ness, and so on.
Is it the "wascally wabbit's" outsize incisors?
The rain-colored fur with its white piping?
His buoyant cruelty and its inventive expression?
The resourcefulness, the abrupt sentiment?
It is, I tell you, all of these things, and more,
more than you or I have the capacity to imagine,
resolving themselves into that one "sensitive chord,"
which may one day come to be a *text* entitled "Bugs."

ACKNOWLEDGMENTS

The author wishes to thank the editors of the *London Review of Books*, where so many of these poems first appeared.

Also, heartfelt thanks to fellow poet friends William Corbett, Michael O'Brien, Robert VanderMolen, and Thom Gunn, posthumously, who read through many of these poems in their early drafts, both for their encouragement and for alerting me to wrong turns in the road. They should in no way be blamed for any wreckage one may encounter along the way.

Also by August Kleinzahler

POETRY

THE HOTEL ONEIRA

SLEEPING IT OFF IN RAPID CITY:
   POEMS, NEW AND SELECTED

THE STRANGE HOURS TRAVELERS KEEP

LIVE FROM THE HONG KONG NILE CLUB: POEMS 1975-1990

GREEN SEES THINGS IN WAVES

RED SAUCE, WHISKEY AND SNOW

LIKE CITIES, LIKE STORMS

EARTHQUAKE WEATHER

ON JOHNNY'S TIME

STORM OVER HACKENSACK

A CALENDAR OF AIRS

THE SAUSAGE MASTER OF MINSK

PROSE

SALLIES, ROMPS, PORTRAITS, AND
   SEND-OFFS: SELECTED PROSE, 2000-2016

MUSIC: I-LXXIV

CUTTY, ONE ROCK: LOW CHARACTERS AND
   STRANGE PLACES, GENTLY EXPLAINED

BEFORE DAWN ON BLUFF ROAD

AUGUST KLEINZAHLER

—

BEFORE DAWN ON BLUFF ROAD

—

SELECTED NEW JERSEY POEMS

—

FARRAR STRAUS GIROUX / NEW YORK

Farrar, Straus and Giroux
18 West 18th Street, New York 10011

Most of the poems in this book originally appeared, some in different form, in the following publications: the *London Review of Books*, *The New Yorker*, *The Threepenny Review*, and *The Times Literary Supplement*. Several of the poems also appeared in the collections *The Hotel Oneira*, *Sleeping It Off in Rapid City*, and *Live from the Hong Kong Nile Club*.

Library of Congress Cataloging-in-Publication Data
Names: Kleinzahler, August, author.
Title: Before dawn on bluff road : selected New Jersey poems ;
    Hollyhocks in the fog : selected San Francisco poems / August Kleinzahler.
Description: First edition. | New York : Farrar, Straus and Giroux, 2017.
Identifiers: LCCN 2016041349 | ISBN 9780374282110 (hardcover) |
    ISBN 9780374715946 (e-book)
Subjects: | BISAC: POETRY / American / General.
Classification: LCC PS3561.L38285 A6 2017b | DDC 811/.54—dc23
LC record available at https://lccn.loc.gov/2016041349

Designed by Quemadura

www.fsgbooks.com
www.twitter.com/fsgbooks
www.facebook.com/fsgbooks

FOR MARSS-SSHALITA,

''I KNEW I'D LEAN BUT I NEVER THOUGHT I'D FALL''

—MEL STREET, "THE DEVIL IN YOUR KISSES
(AND THE ANGEL IN YOUR EYES)," 1976

WHO KNOWS THE PALISADES AS I DO
KNOWS THE RIVER BREAKS EAST FROM THEM
ABOVE THE CITY—BUT THEY CONTINUE SOUTH
—UNDER THE SKY—TO BEAR A CREST OF
LITTLE PEERING HOUSES THAT BRIGHTEN
WITH DAWN BEHIND THE MOODY
WATER-LOVING GIANTS OF MANHATTAN.

  —WILLIAM CARLOS WILLIAMS, "JANUARY MORNING"

INERT GRENADE FOUND IN NUTLEY

  —NEWS BULLETIN FLASHED ACROSS THE SCREEN
  ABOVE THE COUNTER AT PHO'NOMENON NOODLE &
  GRILL, HOBOKEN, NEW JERSEY, JANUARY 6, 2014

CONTENTS

BEFORE DAWN ON BLUFF ROAD

BEFORE DAWN ON BLUFF ROAD

The crow's raw hectoring cry
scoops clean an oval divot
of sky, its fading echo
among the oaks and poplars swallowed
first by a jet banking west
then the Erie Lackawanna
sounding its horn as it comes through the tunnel,
through the cliffs to the river
and around the bend of King's Cove Bluff,
full of timber, Ford chassis, rock salt.

You can hear it in the dark
from beyond what was once the amusement park.
And the wind carries along as well,
from down by the river,
when the tide's just so,
the drainage just so,
the chemical ghost of old factories,
the rotted piers and warehouses:
lye, pig fat, copra from Lever Bros.,
formaldehyde from the coffee plant,

dyes, unimaginable solvents—
a soup of polymers, oxides,

tailings fifty years old
seeping through the mud, the aroma
almost comforting by now, like food,
wafting into my childhood room
with its fevers and dreams.
My old parents asleep,
only a few yards across the hall,
door open—lest I cry?

                         I remember
almost nothing of my life.

LO MEIN

You were still only a child,
I, nineteen, the age of your eldest boy now.
It was the evening of the Marijuana Caper
your eyes first met mine at the China Chalet.
I believe it would have been spring,
early, but days clearly lengthening,
a patch of ice maybe here or there,
pussy willow catkins . . .
We nearly bought it twice that evening,
my father swerving left and right,
Mother, beside him, silent, stiff with fright.
He was mad at something.
Mad, of course, at life, but mad:
only very occasionally, and on this occasion.
They'd dose a man like that these days,
or try. He'd never have stood for it,
nor any of us, who knew the storm he sailed in
and trembled to be on board with him, but still . . .
Your hair was black, or nearly so,
and long for a child's, partway down your back.
Your eyes dark as well, roving, restless,
then, as now, taking in the busy room,
as you fitfully dug through your pile of lo mein.
We hadn't planned to get him stoned.

Improvisation was a habit in that household.
He insisted we put it in his pipe,
to prove that he was right, getting high
was humbug, a notion fools entertain.
Mother hid in the kitchen, out of sight.
It was a longish drive for us of a Sunday,
but not so long as it ordinarily might have been.
His frenzy, that's what would have caught your eye,
the way he went after it, like a dog at a carcass,
scowling over his left shoulder, then his right,
dare a stranger approach to share or take away
the wonton crisps or dumplings, beef
with scallions, shredded pork, whatever floated by—
New Jersey Chinese fare of the day.
It would have thrilled, or frightened, a child
to behold an adult at table quite so wild.
Forty years ago, forty years . . .
You don't remember all that, do you?
How could you? I'm making it up,
the two of us both there at the same time.
It might easily have been true.
If I made it up, it's because it pleases me to.
As you please me, poking through your lo mein,
raising your head nervously to take in the room,
me, and what's doing with the rain.

FAMILY ALBUM

Loneliness—huge, suddenly menacing
and no one is left here who knows me anymore:
the Little League coach,
his TV repair truck and stinking cigars
and Saul the Butcher Man
and the broken arm that fell out of the apple tree,
dead,
dead or gone south to die warm.

The little boy with mittens and dog
posing on the stoop—
he isn't me;
and the young couple, matching polo shirts, ready to pop,
holding their firstborn
four pages on in short-shorts and beatnik top
showing her figure off at sixteen . . .
1955 is in an attic bookcase,
spine cracked and pages falling out.

Willow and plum tree,
green pods from maple whirling down to the sidewalk . . .
Only the guy at the hot dog stand since when
maybe remembers me,
or at least looks twice.

But the smushfaced bus from New York, dropping
them off at night along
these avenues of brick, somber as the dead child
and crimes of old mayors,
lets off no one I know, or want to.

Warm grass and dragonflies—
O my heart.

CLOSING IT DOWN ON THE PALISADES

[September]

Kettles, rain hats—
the small, unopened bottles of Angostura bitters,
its label stained and faded with the years.

The breeze is doing something in the leaves
it hasn't been, not at this hour.
The light, as well.

Early yet for the cicadas,
their gathering rush and ebb.
Too cool,
the sun not high enough.

A cardinal darting among the shadows
in back of the yard,
only at this hour
and again at dusk.

What is it so touching
about these tiny episodes of color
amid the greenery and shadows,
now and at day's end,

that puts to rout all other sentiment?

[October]

The garbage truck compactor is grinding
all twenty-four volumes of the *Encyclopædia Britannica*,
1945 Edition, including Index and Atlas,
along with apple cores, bed linen, ashtrays,
and all that remains of an ailing begonia.

It is raining, not yet light. The wrens
will have put off their convening on the hemlock.
The distant beach homes of Malibu
come strangely to mind, high on the cliffs
overlooking the Pacific,

and how, now and then, after a terrible storm,
the soil beneath washes away, followed
not long after by the house itself, sliding
then crashing to the rocks below, its side tables,
vanities, and clocks licked at

by the gathering foam and, finally, pulled to sea.
Every Saturday they awaken me before dawn,
lights flashing, men shouting, the hydraulic whine
of the compactor as it gnashes away:
desk drawers, yearbooks, sugar bowls.

I shall miss them. I shall miss
the sound of passenger jets overhead
making their descent into Newark in the rain,
before dawn, the first arrivals of the day,
with groggy visitors from Frankfurt, Bahrain.

There is hardly anything left to take—
lamps, a chair, bedspring and mattress.
The last roses still abloom out in the yard.
I can't tell you what kind, pink and white,
the tallest of them six, seven feet high.

Then, that'll be it till spring.
That'll be it till spring.

MEAT

How much meat moves
Into the city each night
The decks of its bridges tremble
In the liquefaction of sodium light
And the moon a chemical orange

Semitrailers strain their axles
Shivering as they take the long curve
Over warehouses and lofts
The wilderness of streets below
The mesh of it
With Joe on the front stoop smoking
And Louise on the phone with her mother

Out of the industrial meadows
They arrive, numberless
Hauling tons of dead lamb
Bone and flesh and offal
Miles to the ports and channels
Of the city's shimmering membrane
A giant breathing cell
Exhaling its waste
From the stacks by the river
And feeding through the night

WHERE GALLUCCIO LIVED

Get all of it, boys,
every brick,
so the next storm blows out
any ghost left with the dust.

In that closet of air the river
wind gnaws at
was where the crucifix hung;
and over there

by the radio and nails,
that's where Galluccio kept
with his busted leg
in an old soft chair

watching TV and the cars
go past.

       Whole floors,
broken up and carted off . . .

Memory stinks,
like good marinara sauce.
You never get that garlic smell
off the walls.

AUBADE ON EAST 12TH STREET

The skylight silvers
and a faint shudder from the underground
travels up the building's steel.

Dawn breaks across this wilderness
of roofs with their old wooden storage tanks
and caps of louvered cowlings

moving in the wind. Your back,
raised hip and thigh
well-tooled as a rounded baluster

on a lathe of shadow and light.

THE HOTEL ONEIRA

That was heavy freight moved through last night,
and has been moving through since I'm back,
settled in again by the Hudson at the Hotel Oneira:
maps on the walls, shelves of blue-and-white Pelicans,
multiple editions of the one epistolary novel by K.,
the curios—my sediment, you might say, my *spattle trail*.

Look at them down there by the ferry slip,
the bridal party, organza, chiffon, and lace, beside themselves,
being wonderful, desperately wonderful, a pastel foam.
Behind them a tug pushes a rusted barge upriver.
Helicopters, small planes, passenger jets above.
They behave, these girls, as if this is their last chance to be thus.

You can feel the rumble of the trains
vibrating up the steel of the hotel's frame.
They move only very late at night, from three or so until dawn,
north along the river and then west.
There is going on just now a vast shifting of inventory
from the one place to another. I can feel it, inside my head.

I find myself going down there, late, behind the highway,
at the base of the cliffs, where the track runs.
Last night, what at first looked like a giant coelacanth

strapped to a flatbed rattled slowly past,
but it was merely the enfoldings of a tarp catching the streetlight.
I remember Uncle Istvan at the lake, unaccountably.

This has been going on quite a lot since I'm here.
How is it that I remember him? I saw him but the one time
and was a very small child, at that:
the madras Bermudas, the foreign, almost spastic gestures?
What is in those railcars is also inside my head,
or I imagine it so—no, not imagine, *know*.

How can one know such a thing with certainty? One knows.
Visitors come by my rooms.
The new one, black-haired Ileanna, I most hate to see go.
It is always when the lights first come on across the river,
late in summer, early in winter,
but always when the lights begin over there,
in the countless apartments, with their cloth napkins and vases.
At first, only the late afternoon sunlight,
glinting off windows as the sun lowers in the skies,
but not long after, that's when the lights begin to come on;
that is when she gathers herself and leaves.
There is a story there, but one I choose not to know.

LATE AUTUMN AFTERNOONS

Red pear leaves take the light at four,
and a patch of brick on the south rear wall
stripped of wisteria: the two reds embering
a little while then dying back into the shadows.
A corner of the afternoon is all,
maybe half an hour, not much more—
October, November . . . the beech tree bare now.

Sunday's blow would have done it.
And always the Interstate out there, like surf,
running up to Boston or south to New York.
The broken-up city across the river,
a used-to-be textile port, gutted.
One good high-rise, an old-style step-back,
the power plant on Point Street,

glowing orange now in sodium light,
highlines feeding out of it, dripping
with porcelain isolators. We watch it every night,
red lights blinking from the three tall stacks,
the staggered sequence of flashing crowns
scaring off the geese and Cessnas.
The turbines and generators roar, never ceasing.

We went inside. We saw it. We heard.
He made us lean underneath and see the flame
through the thick glass, deep in the steel.
And then we went back into the wind,
past the Nightingale Metals truck
and across the bridge on foot. No one saw.
No one knows. The eyes of the beech.

We have examined these afternoons
like a slide taken from a petri dish,
spindles of living matter, degraded, fraying,
taking on new shapes, gray, opalescent.
The red lights in the distance, blinking.
The roar in the boiler house.
The drawn shades.

WHO STOLE THE HORSES
FROM THE INDIANS?

Who stole the horses from the Indians?
my father used to ask.
                          Was it you?
Oh no! I'd pipe. *Not me.*
But my father always knew.

Then there was another game:
Where are you going?

                          To China, I'd announce,
Asbury Park, Hollywood.

*Say hello to Dorothy Lamour. Don't forget
to write.*
            And off I'd spring,
but never fast enough.
He'd catch me by the arm and haul me in.

Where are you going?
my father used to ask when I was grown.

Alaska, I would tell him,
Lisbon, Montreal.

                    You can't,
my father would tell me.
Drifters live that way.

But he was older and I was quick.
You can't, he'd say.
                    And off I'd go.

Where are you going?
my father asks,
                    and now he's old.

Vancouver, I tell him,
San Francisco, Idaho.

He just smiles sadly,
and says hardly anything at all.

SUNDAY NOCTURNE

Red pulse the big jet's lights
in descent.
          The aerial
on the plumber's duplex shakes.

Along these palisades the crowded
grids subside.
          Tonight

even lawyers
and hoods
approach the foothills of reverie.

No pizza slice for the wayfarer
at this hour.
          Get thee to an inn, sport.

And still more jets,
dipping.
          From Dakar,
Akron, and Samoa.
                    A gentleman
in Italian loafers
disembarks.
Tomorrow at one he will bring
profound good news
to a steak joint in Moonachie.

CAT IN LATE AUTUMN

Minou sleeps all day. Old
   soldiers with bum radios
stuck in downtown residence hotels
   see more light than
Minou.
   Sundays,
when rain streams off fire escapes,
   plunging into alleys,
and what little is left of light
   on the street comes off
olive oil cans from Lucca and the groves
   near Córdoba
in a window with pears, dish soap,
   and nuts, Minou
looks nearly dead, a forepaw draped on top
   of his head. He's way
out there, sunk
   deep in the textured rayon
of a buff-colored cushion. His whiskers'
   occasional twitch: you see
the heart jump in his fur
   as he stalks the perimeter
of an enormous dream, rain
   turning so heavy near dusk
night slips in
   without you even noticing.

SILVER GELATIN

He was watching, looking down at the park
from the fourteenth floor, waiting.
There is an hour, an afternoon light
well along into winter.

The angle she made with the pram
as she moved past the fountain
could not possibly be improved upon.
Her black hat,

the fur collar and padded shoulders—
a solitary young domestic,
caught through a net of griseous branches,
is getting the baby home for dinner,

home long before dark.
It is terribly cold.
She leans forward, pushing in haste.
At her own now extreme angle

and with the black coat and hat,
the pram underneath her,
the snow underfoot,
she looks, for all the world, from here,

a broken-off piece of Chinese ideogram
moving across the page.

WINTER BRANCHES

A reticulum of capillaries the full moon
beats through
    the sky late winter
between sunset and dark

more clarifying to the spirit
than the ancient Chinese glazes, tea dust
    plum shade
the celadons from Hangzhou

that take hold of the mind
fastening it
    and when a bird shoots through
between shadow and snow, branch and roof

the heart tracks it
rinsed in a pleasure so distilled
    so exquisite and sharp
as to seem a kind of ecstasy

RED SAUCE, WHISKEY AND SNOW

Ingots of cinnabar and gold
Under a window of snow
Snow-sky, ganglia of dark branches clawing at it
Snow along the Hudson, fastening to bluestone the length of the
　　Palisades
Falling on valleys and abandoned pavilions at the river's northern
　　reaches
The kitchen light almost amber, Dutch Interior light
The little green vase, stone Buddha, indigo cat, all backlit on the
　　windowsill
Through the window wild diagonals of snow
Blowing across planes of snow
Gables and sweeping roofs, shadows, brick, and an enormous
　　crow
The ferry slips through the snow, back and forth to Manhattan
The towers ghostly as it pulls away from shore
A gathering aroma of earth and fruit
As the sauce darkens with the juices of meat, craters and thickens
Somewhere back there, early in the second movement
The clarinet located an emotion, one long forgotten
Then let it go
Drifts have nearly buried the pump house
And a great quiet has covered the swings and jungle gym

The suave bite of oak, an unfastening, a small dull tap at the base
    of the skull
The slow release of sibilants, *O*s and *I*s
Then thunder, muffled, snow thunder, no
A big jet passing by low, hidden in cloud

ON FIRST LOOKING INTO
JOSEPH CORNELL'S DIARIES

The sopressata fée outside of Calfasso's
with the swept-back 'do and blood on her smock
grabs a quick smoke on the sidewalk,
tosses the butt in the gutter then sucks back her lips
till they smack, getting her lipstick right.

                                          Fierce little thing . . .
My freight elevator makes a distant *whump*
then squeals to a stop on one of the floors back there
behind my left ventricle.

                       OUT OF SERVICE
for months, I am at first alarmed then refreshed.

—

What a preposterously springlike day on Anderson Avenue
for the depths of February.

                             You can hear the snow melt
under the parked cars, and the #4 School crossing guard,
burly and mustachioed, reminds me just then
of an elderly Victor McLaglen, a favorite of the children
and somewhat stooped in his waning years
but ever that loyal and gallant pal from *Gunga Din*.

—

Try as I might now for weeks I still cannot find
the space I need to contain the Clorox label
which would go behind and to the right
of the orange box of gelatin stool softeners.

———

There is that and the far larger dilemma,
one that has resisted me and my wiles for year;
to find a distillate or tincture
of daytime TV commercials for the ladies—
Pond's cold cream, say, or diaper rash powders—
then somehow reconstitute and *fashion the flavor*
to a doctor's waiting room and a blue plastic chair
(in the modern Italian design style)
with a splayed, greasy *Mademoiselle*
from the previous June left underneath.

(Oh, but if I could only unknot that one
every arroyo and vista would open up to me.)

I go park awhile outside the boarded-up Dairy Queen
and try to summon Fauré's *Berceuse*.
                                        A gust of wind
rocks the car, just perceptibly,
and then it comes to me, is served up, really:
warm butterscotch syrup and the Little League parade.

———

My *condition* intrudes
and all the air goes right out of me.
It is the bad feeling. I call it *Dolph*.
It smells of roofing tar and makes my pineal gland itch,
itch till it aches.

It spreads into my extremities and lays waste my strength
so that never again will my inventions come to life:

that little green chutney bottle in a field of stars
and the doll's taffeta apron . . .

nor will I ever bathe again with the divine Mavlakapova
in my special Thursday dream.

SNOW IN NORTH JERSEY

Snow is falling along the Boulevard
and its little cemeteries hugged by transmission shops
and on the stone bear in the park
and the WWI monument, making a crust
on the soldier with his chinstrap and bayonet
It's blowing in from the west
over the low hills and meadowlands
swirling past the giant cracking stills
that flare all night along the Turnpike
It is with a terrible deliberateness
that Mr. Ruiz reaches into his back pocket
and counts out eighteen dollars and change for his LOTTO picks
while in the upstairs of a thousand duplexes
with the TV on, cancers *tick   tick   tick*
and the snow continues to fall and blanket
these crowded rows of frame and brick
with their heartbreaking porches and castellations
and the red '68 Impala on blocks
and Joe he's drinking again and Myra's boy Tommy
in the old days it would have been a disgrace
and Father Keenan's not been having a good winter
and it was nice enough this morning
till noon anyhow with the sun sitting up there like a crown
over a great big dome of mackerel sky

but it's coming down now, all right
falling on the Dixon Crucible pencil factory
and on the spur to Bayonne
along the length of the Pulaski Skyway
and on St. Bridget's and the Alibi Saloon
closed now, 'ho dear, I can't remember how long
and lordjesussaveus they're still making babies
and what did you expect from this life
and they're calling for snow tonight and through tomorrow
an inch an hour over 9 Ridge Road and the old courthouse
and along the sluggish gray Passaic
as it empties itself into Newark Bay
and on Grandpa's store that sells curries now
and St. Peter's almost made it to the semis this year
It's snowing on the canal and railyards, the bus barns and trucks
and on the swells in their big houses along the river bluff
It's snowing on us all
and on the three-story fixer-upper off of Van Vorst Park
a young lawyer couple from Manhattan bought
where for no special reason in back of a closet
a thick, dusty volume from the '30s sits open
with a broken spine and smelling of mildew
to a chapter titled "Social Realism"

PORTRAIT OF MY MOTHER IN JANUARY

Mother dozes in her chair,
awakes awhile and reads her book,
then dozes off again.
Wind makes a rush at the house
and, like a tide, recedes. The trees are sere.

Afternoons are the most difficult.
They seem to have no end,
no end and no one there.
Outside the trees do their witchy dance.
Mother grows smaller in her chair.

BLUE AT FOUR P.M.

The burnish of late afternoons
as winter ends—
this sadness coming on in waves is not round
and sweet
as the doleful cello

but jagged, intent
finding out places to get through the way the wind
tries seams
and cracks in the old house, making
the furnace kick on

or the way his trumpet
sharks
through cloud and paradise shoal, nosing
out the dark fillet
to tear apart and drink his own

LATE WINTER MORNING
ON THE PALISADES

Candle in the throat of maple
alive in wet bark
like a soldering flame as the sun lifts
over Manhattan's shoulder,

the yard for a minute, no more,
washed in an antique gold,
a kind of cathedral light filtering down
on squirrels

digging up turf. The earth,
after a fortnight's thaw,
loosens, loosening some more
until a musty bouquet

digs a small trench in us, light
playing on pebbles and clods,
traceries in clay.
                    Suddenly car doors,
jets, and *the brutal slaying in Queens* . . .

Morning rinsing the shadows,
pouring out day.

FROM FDR DRIVE THE CHILDREN
OF WHITMAN GAZE UP

Lavender smoke from the Con Ed stacks
assembles its tufts
into bubbles of thought (viz., the funnies) high
                              over the chilly river
and her bridges,
monuments of clunkish whimsy from an Age of Boom.

For the sky is synchronous this evening;
through the windshield its vistas
exactly right.
                    Yes, and speed too is sweet
at the golden hour,
dipping under viaducts and out
into heraldic light on the bounce

off Citicorp's roof,
the only pentahedron in sight,
up, way up
                high for a street-rooted thing
but kin of sky

as are those puffs wind
fails to scatter

but simply hang there like smudged zeppelins
one might be induced to
think scented

            while small craft higher up

crisscross
aimlessly over the factories and luncheonettes
of Queens,

         clearly beyond this spectacle
and thou,
dreamily seeking your exit.

SELF-PORTRAIT

It was a *lost* dream, a bridges and heights
and headed-home dream, but too long,
far too long and mazy and all the wrong tone.
And then there was that station, so massive,
with its tiers, platforms, girders, and steps,
trains rushing through on the express track,
filled to bursting, commuters illuminated,
each face vivid, highlighted—is that you?—
exasperation, fatigue, concern at the time.
But the time was all wrong; it was late,
way late, the station ready to close.
The subways never close, you say, even in dreams:
empty, only rarely if ever a train, but open.
This was no ordinary station, or dream.

You could see Manhattan in the far distance,
big towers beyond the raggedy miles
of tenements, viaducts, frozen playgrounds.
Like the view from the nor'easter headed south
as it winds its way around the Bronx,
right before it dips down into the tunnel.
But this would have had to be in Queens.
At the start it was a plane I was headed for,
headed for that morning from quite another town.

This must be the old *train to the plane*,
the one that lets you off way out by Kennedy.
But that got shut down years ago.
Now I was far from anything, Jersey especially.
I always head back to Jersey in a pinch.

My two suitcases were gone as well, both black,
one large, one small. My shoes too, also black.
There I was, lost, weaving left and right,
pitiful as a *cucaracha* caught out in the light.
Way down there in the bowels with the gated-up
shoeshine, burger, and newsstands, a cop, a drunk.
But a barbershop of sorts still open and lit
and oddly partitioned into three distinct rooms:
one with a man fitting rubber skin skulls
onto mannequin heads; the next a barber
fussily attending to three bald heads;
the next what could only be a tiny morgue,
but with those very same heads from the barber's,
only this time like death masks of Renaissance popes.

That's when I ran into this burly black guy,
security or some kind of station chief.
He was short with me for being there but nice enough
and led me on a search for my two bags.
Through horrible rooms: bodies, gunnysacks,
leavings from some old and gruesome jumble sale.

—The two last rooms on earth, I heard myself say.
And still no bags, but when I looked down
there were my shoes, back on my feet again,
except each from a different pair. Odd, that,
but I was plenty glad to have them on,
stuck by myself in the middle of nowhere
with the station shutting down for the night
and who knows what waiting out there in the shadows.

Somehow it had gotten to be dawn.
I found myself standing up to my ankles in weeds
with rusted fenders and a torn-down fence,
Manhattan sticking up there in the distance.
Lots of birds, planes too, out of Kennedy.
When two ugly-looking kids were headed my way.
Didn't like how this was shaping up at all.
If I had to bolt, the weeds would hold me back.
But they turned out to be sweet, bewildered boys,
in wonderment at my simply standing there.
I believe I had on a flannel shirt, a plaid,
sun igniting the wet dark smells of earth.
It was all so eerily gentle and strange
I might as well have been Captain Cook in the Marquesas.

16

The creases in the schoolboy's pegged wool slacks
blow flat against his ankles
as he puffs uphill in the Bronx. The day
is raw and new. He didn't do his Latin.

Below and to the east smoke braids
and drifts further east. Levering and stoking
out there grown men in coveralls slog through
the dead hours, while in their lunch pails

bologna sweats. A bird is in the schoolboy's head:
Shelley's skylark. Ha, Mr. Sensitive in Breeches
never lurched uptown on the El with squads
of plump domestics lost in romance comics

and down each night,
past the Stella D'oro cookie factory, its sigh-fetching smells.
Oh, if only his soul could take flight, just this once,
and drift far, far away to a meadow

commanding a height over the Bay of Naples.
Girls would be there waiting, in bright cotton dresses
pulled up just past the knee,
offering him warm glances and sweet things to eat.

And here, in this very place,
our unhappy young man, nearly about to burst with yearning,
here amid the daisies and beguiling strangers,
will flare and then perish exquisitely.

SHOOT THE FREAK

Shoot the freak   Cold wind, boardwalk nearly empty   *You know*
   you wanna
A cluster of hip-hop Lubavitch punks, shirttails out, talking
   tough   *You shoot him*
he don't shoot back   Keeper flatties thrashing in buckets, out on
   the pier
Shoot the freakin' freak   a regular family of man, fishing for fluke
and blues in that wind   *How you gonna build memories*
   Everything shut

or broken down and carted off   *Let the lady have a try*
   SpongeBob, Spook-A-Rama,
Luna Park   *Shoot 'im in the head*   the Mighty Atom,
   Thunderbolt, Wonder Wheel
He likes it when you shoot'im in the face   Surf Hotel, Astroland,
   Shatzkin's
knishes.   *A real live human target*   "Hungry for Fun," fried
   clams
Everybody's gonna   "Bump yo' ass, bump bump bump yo' ass"
You know you wanna   You know you wanna   You know you
   wanna
And that's when we spot him, *him*, 120 million records sold
   worldwide

walking across the sand   "It's him, it's him" Like a god, with that
    hair
What does he do to keep it like that   Looking good, still, tall,
    slim, creased slacks
handmade Italian boots, a black goddess on his arm, like an older
    version of that chick
on Miles's *Sorcerer* album, wow   The camera crew running all
    around them, frantic
He's waving his arm toward the ocean, telling her how it used to be
how it used to be when he was growing up close by in Brighton
    Beach
OhmyGodOhmyGod   "Sweet Caroline," "Holly Holy," "You
    Don't Bring Me Flowers"
the duet with you-know-who, the two of them in the choir together
    at Lincoln High
the 1992 Christmas special, the White House concert, the time he
    met Lady Di
("a great person, just a fabulous person, a real human being")
I mean, how good is this, really, I mean really, seriously, how good
    is this

THE DOG STOLTZ

The dog Stoltz pushed his paw pads into my neck,
the warm, beaten leather deep under my chin,
and let slip the one paw to up near my mouth
with all the filth of the many blocks we trod,
together trod, a well-moistened, adenoidal sound,
part sigh and part growl, coming out of him,
transported, he seemed, in a slow-motion delirium
as I tickled his chest and behind his ear
when he just then told me he'd tear out my throat,
looked me in the eye and smiled, best as a dog can,
then turned ruminative and spoke once more:
—*I simply have to knock off that essay on Sassoon.*
This would have been Sassoon the war poet, understand.
Dogs cannot write. My mother told me this.
As for his talk, well, I took no special notice.
His love of the war poets was well known.
Stoltz would have been part bull and something else.
Two friends walked by just then, handily as these things go,
and inquired of us sitting down there on the stoop,
not even, a doorway merely, along a busy street,
how went the day and what pursuits was I attending;
but what interested the two of them most
were the tergiversations of the dog Stoltz,
first beast, then scholar, then abject and adored.

(Say, who among us does not care to be undressed?)
He was not really my dog, you see, and of this made note,
but were glad as well at my having a new dog in my life.
It was a busy stretch of pavement, Amsterdam maybe,
or Broadway, or farther down, just south of Chelsea.
I can tell you it was the West Side, of that I'm certain,
and it was mild, springlike, a few drops in the air.
The friends passed along and the dog Stoltz slept.
He was not my dog, you know. He simply followed me out
of what can only have been a very fine home,
such were his graces, his recondite tastes.
But he was a killer too, and rather smelled.
I cannot accommodate another animal now, please understand.
I am between places. I will yearn for Stoltz, but no.

1975

Even the crickets are unnerving me tonight,
and the smell of camphor in the warm room
worse still; my woolens will outlast me.
Home again, from points north, west,
a suitcase full of useless books and no prospects.
There's a folk song that goes like that:
insipid—pathetic, really—without the music.
This appears to be a condition I shall not escape,
a gravitational field to be suffered through all my days,
like some wayward, doomed alien.
At least the folks are asleep. Getting along in years,
they shrug. A shrug means peace.
The stomach knows, when the clams are bad, or worse.
Perhaps that is truly the site for love,
or where love takes root, finally, and sets up shop.
I had imagined something much less uncomfortable.
The dirty aureole across the Hudson is New York.
Jets sink into it. Here, on the cliffs opposite,
trees whisk themselves. The wind freshens for rain.
Even George Washington, on the lam from Howe,
hid out here. He ate and ran
south. Ask any ghost along the Hackensack.
It's late, very late; that I do know.
Mother's bought new bed linen for the occasion,
described on the package as "duck egg blue,"
so clean and cool I could be afloat on a lake.

GOING

The old people are dying,
they're falling apart piece by piece
like vintage Studebakers,
but the docs keep pumping diuretics and prednisone
into them, doing valve jobs,
so they go slow, terribly slow.

They're talking tumor,
they're talking colon and biopsy
over biscuit tortoni and tea.
                              The doctors
are butchers, and as for the kids—
selfish insensitive little shits.

Check out Sinatra and Reagan,
dewlaps trembling in the wee small hours,
glued to *I Love Lucy* reruns
as the Secret Service men doze.
They own cliffs and enormous stretches
of desert, those two—
shopping centers, distilleries.

Lucy is dead, boys, give it up:
Desi, the Duke, and Ava,

dust:
      even little Sammy's
checked out.

All the great ones, the class acts,
taking their bows
          or history.

WATCHING DOGWOOD BLOSSOMS FALL
IN A PARKING LOT OFF ROUTE 46

Dogwood blossoms drift down at evening
    as semis pound past Phoenix Seafood

and the Savarin plant, west to the Turnpike,
    Paterson or hills beyond.

The adulterated, pearly light and bleak perfume
    of benzene and exhaust

make this solitary tree and the last of its bloom
    as stirring somehow after another day

at the hospital with Mother and the ashen old ladies
    lost to TV reruns flickering overhead

as that shower of peach blossoms Tu Fu watched
    fall on the riverbank

from the shadow of the Jade Pavilion,
    while ghosts and the music

of yellow orioles found out the seam of him
    and slowly cut along it.

POETICS

I have loved the air above ShopRite Liquors
on summer evenings
better than the Marin hills at dusk
lavender and gold
stretching miles to the sea.

At the junction, up from the synagogue
a weeknight, necessarily
and with my father—
a sale on German beer.

Air full of living dust:
bus exhaust, airborne grains of pizza crust
wounded crystals
appearing, disappearing
among streetlights and unsuccessful neon.

TANKA TOYS: A MEMOIR

The planet may have tilted, if only a hint
when the shelf of cloud burned angrily
before dusk
         jack-o'-lantern stuff

her hair the color of her coat
fall wear

    —

The wet stain her bathing suit left
on the bench
            the shape of Bolivia
drying, drying into atolls
Ursa Minor, a thumbprint

    —

It was at Herbie's place, no
Pinckney's, she showed us her pubes
and long shadow of thigh

The fresh linens smelled so sunnily like
What did the lady on TV call it
An orchard of some kind

—

Sure it's like staring
out the window, Johnny
sure

but with fly eyes
and sidewise

—

When Pappy and Mahoney left
for dinner and a show

I was soooo-a-LONE
there in the doorway, sore way
of being the phone ringing

It was summer again and green

—

You do turkey, baby, I like peas
snap beans, oyster sauce, fuzzy

blond roux

—

The clues to my being:
the bloody windsprint
the mashie niblick hanging
from a willow

the retreating aria

—

The way the spaldeen jumped left
instead of right

and died on your square of sidewalk
that Friday afternoon so long ago
That's all you need to know

—

Oh, I was freed
freed, I tell you

kneeling, teething

chopchopchopping
like a tractor piston

like an outboard coughing up lake

AS YOU NEVER BOTHERED
TO RETURN MY CALL

What I had wanted was to be chaste,
sober, and uncomfortable
for a sprawling episode on a beach somewhere
dirty, perennially out of fashion;
let the smell of cocoa butter drive deep memory wild
as the sun went down, a parti-colored blur,
examined through a bottle of pop
some kid gave up on only halfway through
and left to go warm in the sand.

The train ride would be long and hot,
and you, you've had it with men.
Me . . .
        I'm sickened by the pronoun.
Tenderness seems as far away as Sioux City
and besides, it would have cost too much.
But you should have called,

if only since a preposterous little episode like this
is just the stuff to scare off extra friends,
like soaking their laps with corrosive fizz.
And us . . .
        What an impertinence, *us*.

We could have played gin rummy and taken a stroll
into town or along the boardwalk, maybe,
             with dear old Godzilla,
the first one, the best one, the 1954 one,
reprising his role this one last time, raising himself up
over the horizon at dusk,
and hurrying us to a place we never would have
dreamt of
          going.

STORM OVER HACKENSACK

This angry bruise about to burst
on City Hall
will spend itself fast
so fluid and head may build again.

But for a moment the light
downtown
            belongs someplace else,
not here
or any town close.

Look at the shoppers, how palpable
and bright
against the gathering dark
like storied figures in stereoscope.

This is the gods' perpetual light:
    clarity
  jeopardy
            change.

ART & YOUTH

Pliny said these lights in the grass are stars:
a man walking home from his day's labor
needn't lift his head skyward to tell the signs.
Before the heavens were busy with Sputniks
and idiot beeps that say *hey!* from far-off worlds
we ran at the lights with jars. We ran and ran
until nothing was left of our bodies to spend.

An ache so sweet was born those nights
in the heat, in the grass, at summer's waning
that we try for it years later in the dance
of lust and lust's passing.
                        Poor Swinburne,
dithery and gallant in great drafty rooms,
would have had this ache flogged back into him,
but the heart is soon corrupted
and love's accoutrements grow fierce.

WHERE SOULS GO

No telling where: down the hill
and out of sight—
soapbox derby heroes in a new dimension.
Don't bother to resurrect them
unless some old newsreel clip
catches them shocked
with a butter knife in the toaster.
Countless snaps and episodes in space
once you hit the viewfinder that fits.
It's a lie anyway, all Hollywood—
the Mind is a too much thing
cleansing itself like a great salt sea.
Rather, imagine them in the eaves

among pigeons
or clustered round the D train's fan
as we cross the bridge to Brooklyn.
And make that Friday night
July say. We are walking past
the liquor store to visit our love.
Two black boys are eating Corn Doodles
in the most flamboyant manner possible.
She waits, trying

to have the best song on as we arrive.

The moon is blurred.

Our helicopters are shooting at field-workers.

The Mets are down 3-1 in the sixth.

GREEN RIVER CEMETERY: SPRINGS

Strange to be among them in the noon sun
with their fabulous night histories,
the welter and crush of downtown tableaux
above Second Avenue or at the Hotel Earle,
honeycomb of lambent episode.

Big silence in the midday heat
except for insect whir and a passing car.
You imagine them under the sandy ground,
under the slate and granite markers,
and pretend to hear, faintly at first,

as if through the woods at night,
the stream of delicious talk,
the rages, dishing, and whispered come-ons,
the posturing and retort
at that murderous cocktail party, the fifties,

Speed and Nerve presiding,
right before it blew into a camp B-movie
cavalcade of car wrecks, lithium,
and broken hearts
                    (soundtrack by Schoenberg
and Elmer Bernstein). The afterglow of them:

neon on a sunny day—

                        celluloid in flames,
the fried image and random splice,
wild parabolas, butchery.

THE OLD SCHOOLYARD IN AUGUST

The welling of cicadas in the green
afternoon before the storm
catches on some inner ratchet along with the leaves
so dark and dense in the fading light
their color washes into surrounding air.

And when the first drops pock the dust
of the ball field next to the school,
it is not a piercing aria
of iridescent jellyfish parachuting upward
but darkness

spreading, troweled across the diaphragm.
Every breath drags through it,
bringing in its wake a bewilderment
of fire trucks, galoshes,
the taste of pencils and Louis Bocco's ear

torn off by the fence in a game of salugi.

THE HEREAFTER

At the gates of the Hereafter,
a rather drab affair, might as well be a union hall
in south Milwaukee, but with shackled
sweating bodies along the walls,
female, chiefly, and not at all miserable,
straining like bored sultanas at their fetters,
each of them singing a separate song.
A Semitic chap—the greeter, I suppose—
gives me the quick once-over
and most amused he seems to be. Has me figured.
Not unlike a gent I met only last week,
a salesman at a stereo shop on Broadway.
—*So*, he says. Nothing more.
—*Sew buttons*, says I, in a cavalier tone
and why not.
                        Ushers me into a tiny cinema,
a two-seater, really quite deluxe,
a great big Diet Coke in the cupholder,
fizzing away.
                        —*OK?* he asks.
I nod and the film unrolls.
A twenty-million-dollar home movie it is,
featuring yours truly: at the foot
of the stairs with the dog, mounting

Josette in a New Smyrna love nest,
a fraught kitchen showdown with Mom,
the suicide, car wreck, home run.
You know what these things are like:
the outlandish hairdos, pastel bathroom fixtures.
The editing is out of this world,
the whole shebang in under an hour:
the air-raid drill on Wednesday morning,
1957, when Tito wet his pants;
there I am, beside myself with laughter,
miserable little creature.
The elemental, slow-motion machinery
of character's forcing house.
Even with all the fancy camera angles,
jump cuts, and the rest,
might as well be a chain of short features:
Animal Husbandry, *Sexual Hygiene*,
Lisboa by Night . . .
What a lot of erections, voidings, pretzels,
bouncing the ball against the stoop.
She really did love you, all along.
These jealousies and rages of yours,
like a disgusting skin condition
that never entirely goes away.
You, you . . .
What catalogs of failure, self-deception . . .
And then the lights come back on,

Likewise the choir's splintered polyphony,
with its shards of *Sprechstimme*, the Ronettes, whatnot,
and in the air around us
something like the odor of a freshly spent cartridge,
when my minder asks brightly,
                              —How about another Coke?

A HISTORY OF WESTERN MUSIC: CHAPTER 63

(WHITNEY HOUSTON)

They follow you around the store, these power ballads,
you and the women with their shopping carts filled with eggs,
cookies, 90 fl. oz. containers of antibacterial dishwashing liquid,
buffeting you sideways like a punishing wind.

You stand, almost hypnotized, at the *rosticceria* counter
staring at the braised lamb shanks, the patterns
those tiny, coagulated rivulets of fat make,
both knees about to go out from under you.

—*Can I help you, sir?*
No, no, thank you, I'm afraid not . . .

It's mostly the one woman who writes these things,
a petite, almost perpetually somber brunette
in her LA studio, undecorated, two cats,
traffic coursing up and down the boulevard outside,

curtains drawn against the unrelenting sun.
Because of your *unconventional* lifestyle
you have been shopping among women your entire life,
young mothers and matrons,

almost no other males around except staff and seniors,
the old men squinching their eyes, scowling at the prices.
What sort of life have you led
that you find yourself, an adult male of late middle age,

about to weep among the avocados and citrus fruits
in a vast, overlit room next to a bosomy Cuban grandma
with her sparkly, extravagant eyewear?
It's good that your parents are no longer alive.

It's a simple formula, really: verse, verse, chorus
(and don't take too long to get there),
verse, chorus, bridge, solo, if any,
chorus (good chance of key modulation here, really gets 'em)—

electric keyboard, soaring guitar, likely a string part or two.
There's no telling how much that woman is worth,
a "misunderstood Jewish girl" from Van Nuys.
How would one go about making love to someone like that,

sitting alone in her studio all day, shades drawn, two cats,
writing these songs of tortured love,
up to the tips of her waders in self-immolation,
often keeping at it well into the night?

Céline Dion, Cher, Michael Bolton, Faith Hill, Toni Braxton—
knocking you back one after another, all morning and afternoon,
at least until the men arrive after work. I don't know why.
Perhaps it has to do with the "emotional nature" of women.

You, you're breathing all funny, nearly paralyzed.
But there's one song they almost never play
and I'll tell you why: it's the one Dolly Parton wrote,
not the brunette, but it's not Dolly who's doing the singing,

it's the one who just died. Because if they played that one,
it wouldn't be just you dying in aisle #5.
All the girls would be dropping out there like it was sarin gas
pouring from the speakers up there hidden behind the lights.

ACKNOWLEDGMENTS

The author wishes to thank the editors of the *London Review of Books*, where so many of these poems first appeared.

Also, heartfelt thanks to fellow poet friends William Corbett, Michael O'Brien, Robert VanderMolen, and Thom Gunn, posthumously, who read through many of these poems in their early drafts, both for their encouragement and for alerting me to wrong turns in the road. They should in no way be blamed for any wreckage one may encounter along the way.